Inspiration FROM CONNIE'S CORNER

2nd Edition

CONNIE REDEN

authorHOUSE

AuthorHouse™
1663 Liberty Drive
Bloomington, IN 47403
www.authorhouse.com
Phone: 833-262-8899

Published by AuthorHouse 10/28/2023

ISBN: 979-8-8230-1530-1 (sc)
ISBN: 979-8-8230-1529-5 (e)

Library of Congress Control Number: 2023918282

Print information available on the last page.

Any people depicted in stock imagery provided by Getty Images are models, and such images are being used for illustrative purposes only.
Certain stock imagery © Getty Images.

This book is printed on acid-free paper.

Connie Reden

Author

Connie began writing Connie's Corner as a monthly ministry that satisfied her need to share feelings, thoughts, and testimonies with others about a wondrous God. He constantly inspires her to remind us of his promises. Though she is a Black Catholic, the word catholic means universal, therefore, she believes all Christians have confidence in the same God no matter the denomination. Our God will not pick any one religion for his heaven.

Her early education began 77 years ago with the Oblate Sisters of Providence, the first Black order of nuns in the United States. Her faith is a result of the nuns and a family rich in history and accomplishments. Both expected Connie to do her best in life. Her family fought for its right to be, and fought for her right to be whoever she wanted to be. Love and justice became who she has been.

This collection of readings is a result of God's inspiration and Connie's family always encouraging her to have faith in the Maker. Every experience was to create a strong inner person and help others to know God loves us all. All people are struggling to make it to heaven. Whatever your faith, all roads lead to peace and love for one another.

May her writings transport you to a world of understanding the reality of love. We are all flowers in God's garden that have beauty and purpose. May God bless all who read this book and may he keep his arms tightly around you on this journey called **LIFE**.

Dedicated to my daughter, Krystal, my son-in-law Lance,
my grandsons, Jerrell, Landon, and Langston
and all others I love.

Introduction

A bonfire became an electric lamp inside of a tall building built on a high hill. It overlooked the sea. This is now what we call a lighthouse. The light guides sailors away from dangerous waters. It is a beacon to remind mariners to keep their eyes open. Safety and security are symbols of the light and the knowledge of a safe passage.

I want you to come to Connie's lighthouse. Instead of a towering light, my lighthouse is filled with pages of enlightenment. My lighthouse provides security, safety, faith, and love through words. The words of my lighthouse may bring these to your heart, mind and soul.

Come to my lighthouse and the scenery of words will make you feel **GREAT**!

Contents

III. WHAT MATTERS

IV. IMAGERY

V. LEARNING

VI. MY WORLD

I

FAITH TO SHARE

Good Morning!

Did you rush to have your cup of coffee this morning?

How do you like it? With sugar, sugar and cream, or just plain black?

You feel stimulated by the caffeine and think you can make it for the day.

If at work, you may feel a little sluggish so back to a cup of coffee you go.

What a shame that coffee is your stimulant after you rise in the morning?

Let me tell you something. I have a better stimulant than coffee to keep you going for the day.

I know you know his name. Many people do.

His name is Jesus and with a morning prayer you have the best stimulant to make the day delightful.

You can still have your cup of coffee, but say a prayer of thanks first, then you'll have a double stimulant for the day.

Waking Up

As a little girl, I remember I said a prayer on my knees before I got into bed. Do you remember the prayer? **"Now I lay me down to sleep, I pray the Lord my soul to keep. If I should die before I wake I pray the Lord my soul to take."** This is a prayer as adults we have not said in years. But it is a prayer of relevance. Everyday we awake is a gift and our soul was not taken.

When awaking in the morning, we usually view a bright sun, a blue sky with soft clouds floating to their new destinations. Sometimes we awaken to gray skies that may indicate some kind of precipitation might cover the ground. However, a new day appears before our very eyes. We laid down for the night and awakened to a day of wonder. While getting ready for the new day, we sometimes forget to say "Thank you, Lord." We forget that this day is a gift from God. The new day's gift gives us a chance to do better than the day before. We don't want to make the same mistakes of the previous day.

If we review the day before, there are things that we could have done better. The choice of words could have been better said. Our actions toward another could have shown more kindness. Sharing and loving may not have been part of our day's agenda. The day was only about **us**. We didn't take a minute to thank our Creator for being alive. Even our birthdays are a celebration of God's annual gift to us. We can look back and know the things we did and didn't do. We need to grasp how much God has done for us. We are not seeing the roots of grass. We are still above ground. One thing we can say in the morning is "Thank you, Lord." We can even repent for the wrongs we did as he gives us our daily bread. As my sister always says each day is "Surprise, surprise, surprise! What a wonderful surprise to see a new day."

Faith and Courage

Christians die for their faith. The eleven apostles most certainly were put to a savage death because of teaching and maintaining the faith through all their ordeals. Peter, Andrew, Phillip, Thaddeus, Bartholomew, Simon were crucified. James, son of Alpheus was stoned and his brains bashed out. Judas Iscariot killed himself for his betrayal of Christ. Thomas, Matthias, and Matthew were speared to death and John was the only apostle who died of old age. I question myself as to whether I would have the courage to die for God. What a question!

Some theologians say if we have faith, it will give us courage. I believe each of us could become a martyr as we strengthen our faith through prayer and positive actions. I am not sure I have developed that much faith yet, but I will never know until something happens. I believe God reveals our courage in a split second when faith is challenged. I want to respond to the question with great assurance, but now, I still have doubts.

I ask God to reveal things to me, but I need to sit in a quiet place to hear and see in my mind his revelations. **Wow!** This question of will I die for God I ask myself all the time. The answer has not been revealed in my prayers. Yet, God has a way of revealing what needs to be revealed at the right time. To answer the question proposed, I have no answer. This question requires patience that seems to be a waiting game. But using the burning bush as a symbol of endurance and strength, my faith will not be consumed if martyrdom is God's plan.

A life of faith and courage are not just about moments, but about one's entire life. It is our obituary to our steps to salvation. No matter our crosses, we can transcend them to do unseen things for God. Questions may arise to determine our capacity to make sacrifices, but God knows our fears and helps us to conquer them. Let's find that quiet place to hear his words of courage in our minds that gives us that courage to say, "I will die for you, Lord."

He Came

The winter months bring cold temperatures and winds that chills to the bone. In the month of December I think of the Baby Jesus being born in a manger. The average winter temperature in Bethlehem is usually about 47 degrees, but for the month of January the temperatures are colder. Whether Jesus was born in December or January, it was cold. Can you imagine the frosty temperatures and winds whipping outside the stable on the day he was born? Yet, a star shone in the sky indicating the place where he was born. Now let's think about Jesus being born today.

If a newspaper or a newsflash told us today Jesus was born in a stable, would we rush to the stable, or just change the channel and place the newspaper in the trash? Would we take the time to travel with blankets to give to the Holy Family? Just think about this for a moment. Would we be too relaxed or too busy to make the journey? Would we be the magi with gifts to honor his birth? I fear that we would not. He was being groomed by his heavenly father to make a magnificent sacrifice for us. We sometimes celebrate Christmas without sharing the true meaning of his birth.

I bring this thought to you because we forget sometimes why Jesus came into the world as a human. Bearing all the pains and emotions we feel. Yet, he never forgets to give us comforting grace and blessings he provides for us daily. We don't give to him as we give so graciously to others on Christmas. But after the holiday, our first thought is what we owe in bills. We can be as frigid as the winter temperatures and as flighty as the ferocious winds when it comes to giving.

We don't always have to give money to be a giver. We can speak with words of personal wisdom, smile with the warmth of inner understanding, share prayers for a peaceful humanity, walk with confidence with the knowledge of Jesus. We also recognize we are all God's children. Live the reason for Christmas every day. Keep the cold outside and solemnize the warmth of the Holy Spirit.

How Strong Is Our Faith

Everyday our faith is being tested. We must keep in mind how Jesus resisted temptation. After he had been baptized he went into the desert for 40 days. Our first question is could we have gone into the desert for such a long period of time without food or water? His enemy came first with a temptation for the physical need for food. The enemy's second temptation was to put God to a test and the final temptation was to bow down to the enemy. But Jesus scoffed at all the temptations using the words from Scripture to defeat the enemy. Jesus had faith that his Father would protect him. How strong is our faith that God will protect and deliver us from evil?

There are stories in the Bible that verifies persons having strong faith in God. Think of Daniel who was placed in a den of lions. His enemies persuaded King Darius to punish him because he prayed to his God every day instead of to the king. When Daniel was placed in the den his faith took over. The lions' mouths were closed. Daniel was protected and delivered.

Shadrach, Meshach, and Abednego refused to worship the idols of the king and were placed in a fiery oven, but God placed an angel in the furnace so the three would not burn. They knew their God would deliver them and King Nebuchadnezzar was left startled and a believer that their God was powerful.

The characters mentioned above faced death, yet remained faithful to God and were delivered. How strong is our faith? Can we speak and stand against evil and know God is our Great Protector and Deliverer? Do we run away from confrontations instead of running to God? Seems to me we are cowardly when it is time to face challenges. We have a tendency to run in the wrong direction. If we are being tested are we wearing the armor of God as described in the Bible? We better put it on because **"If God brings you to it, God will bring you through it."**

Take Time

When I moved to Blue Springs, Missouri I received a daily morning greeting text from Yolanda She never missed a day even now that I'm living in Elk Grove, California. This has been almost two years of greetings seven days a week.Yolanda is truly my Sister in Faith. She is a member of Our Lady of Kibeho in Chicago, Illinois and a member of the gospel choir. Her kind gesture to think of others daily, gives a person inspiration, a smile or a laugh. I start the day with a positive mindset from my God and from Yolanda. Not one day has she missed even when I was hospitalized for various conditions. To me this is a sacrifice of time. Her choice of words for each greeting varies from one day to another. I have never received the same greeting twice.

I respond to these morning greetings with positive remarks, but the question arises, "Will I do something special for someone today?" Then I remember my Prayer Partners, Julia and Joann, who are also members of Our Lady of Kibeho (formerly Holy Name of Mary). We pray together everyday at 6:00 p.m. Chicago time. We pray for each other and for everyone on our prayer list everyday. When we have to miss a day we pray separately to ensure our prayer line is unbroken, The deceased Margaret Green and I began being Prayer Partners, Julia joined us and JoAnn joined us later.

Finding prayer time is a small sacrifice compared to the sacrifice of Jesus Christ. But my Sister in Faith and my Prayer Partners take time daily to pray for others and the world. We sometimes take for granted the sacrifice Jesus made for us. Have you given someone a telephone call who is isolated and alone? Have you given something to the beggars on the corner or said a prayer for them? Giving is a sacrifice and the blessings are many. You can easily forget all you have received. I love my Sister in Faith and my Prayer Partners. We are trying to be good Christians. A Bible quote from God is **"I will pour out blessings so great you won't have enough room to take it in!"** Giving has great returns. Try it!

When I Pray

I don't know if you remember when your grandmother and her friends would create a quilt together. Each person would add a square shape of material stretched over a frame so each quilter had a section to complete. They all seemed to begin in the middle and sewed outward to the edges. The frame became smaller as the sewers came closer to the edges. The cloth was stretched out on the frame and stuffing was placed between them and then hand sewn together. When I am trying to have quiet time my mind rambles like the various picture patterns of a quilt. The quilt patterns are the mental gymnastics scouring in my head. I tell my brain "Stay focused", but there is still rambling from one thought to another.

Sometimes when I am lying down and saying my rosary I'm still saying, "Stay focused" and find I have fallen asleep. I awoke to notice my rosary entangled in my night clothes. One time I was praying for someone and remembered how I needed to mop the kitchen floor. The next thing I knew I was mopping the kitchen floor instead of praying for that person. Another time, I was trying to pray when I thought about a song the choir was going to sing. I said, "Lord, I'm trying to pray but there is too much going on in my head. My mind is jumping and it's beginning to frustrate me." I even thought about getting on my knees but I knew I wouldn't be able to get up without help. Plus, my knees were not able to hold my upper weight. "Lord, help me! I don't want to be disrespectful to you as my mind is wondering about so many unimportant things. What can I do?"

Finally, it came to me. All those things I was thinking about could be thought about later. I kept calling the name of Jesus. As I kept calling his name a peace came over me as if he said, "Peace be with you." I began to petition the Lord to keep my family and friends safe and to thank him for his blessing bestowed upon us. There were so many things I wanted to pray for, but I thought God might say, "Time out, Sister Girl." But I was able to complete my prayers because there was the inner peace I needed. He gave me that peace in an instant and I was able to pray.

The evil one does not want us to pray. He puts all kinds of constraints before us to make us fail. But goodness and evil cannot exist in the same space. So, call God's name. Call the name of Jesus and the evil one will depart. He's chicken when it comes to our Mighty God. Our mind can be at peace because God's quilt is our blanket of love, mercy, and safety.

Seven Days

There are seven days in the week and each day's name had meaning to ancient people. What does it mean to us? Sunday seems to mean a day of rest and going to church on Sunday and Saturday seems to remind us to go grocery shopping, doing necessary repairs around the house, or family entertainment together. The rest of the week means working for someone or working for oneself for eight hours or more. Possibly, there is only one day given to God the Creator.

Many people cannot give God more than the hour they spend in church on Sunday. I wonder if the appearance in church is for show or a deep conviction that we need spiritual healing. This healing, for those who believe, is a pathway to salvation. Think how much faith we place in medical doctors to heal us. Pain within our bodies is so excruciating we search for a healing and a cure from the medical doctor. What if the doctor says, "I'm sorry I don't know if I can cure you, but I'll do everything to make you comfortable." What do we do? What can we do?

The best physician I know, who has all the medical degrees you can think of, is the man who lives high in the sky. His healing power can reach down to ease pain and cure what cannot be cured on this earth. Prayer is a powerful means of getting an appointment. No telephone number or fax number is required. No expensive Western Union telegraph communication is needed. Just call his name and he'll be there to comfort you mentally, physically, and spiritually. When we see his works, we will decide to spend more time with him.

God Within Us

My prayer partners and I pray together everyday and we read from *Living Faith, a* daily devotional booklet. After reading an article written by Sister Bridget Haase, Order of Saint Ursula. It was a reminder of a statement she wrote about Saint Paul. My prayer partners and I remarked about this statement "being temples of God". My thoughts brought me to think about pregnancy. This is a special time for a woman who holds in her womb life that is nourished from her body. The life she carries, grows rapidly and is delivered with pain, yet a new life begins.

With my prayer partner as my sounding board, I stated a woman's pregnancy is like being a temple of God. We are all pregnant with God living within us while his love grows and grows within us. Throughout our lives there is nourishment from him every day and as we pray a delivery date comes. This pregnancy is life within us all, both men and women. The love of God that continually grows within us and is delivered without pain. We nurture his love by honoring him just as a woman nurtures life in her womb. His love is "our daily bread".

Sometimes we forget we are carrying a spiritual life inside of us as we go about our daily lives. We need to be reminded that we are temples of God and we become reflections of his goodness. When we pray our pregnancy causes a continuous readiness for our delivery date. We are all pregnant with this spirit who never fails us. We are nourished by his internal presence. He nourishes us by allowing us life and as our delivery date nears without pain. He will call our names to enter our eternal home. **Oh, happy day!**

Time

I am aging and doctor appointments are many. I need every kind of doctor to keep me moving. The joints of my body ache as I pull myself from bed in the morning. Time is like a mild breeze passing over our bodies as our hair grays and our skin wrinkles. The breezes continue to pass, but then comes the big wind with the assistance of gravity pulling our skin in one direction, DOWN! Time seems to bring us to an end. We know that time is measured by the equipment we use, such as clocks. This is our way of measuring the minutes, hours, and days passing. Getting older also seems to mean aging as fast as a spinning wheel spins yarn.

I am so thankful my God does not age. He remains the same as he watches over me during my lifetime. I figure if he did age he would wither away and then who would I have to provide and protect me? I am very much aware that time has no end, but my time is limited. My life is limited based on the decision God makes to lengthen or shorten my life. Time has no beginning or end. When God calls me his voice might be a thunderous roar to loudly say "Connie, it's time." Maybe it may be a soft whisper cuddling my ears saying, "It's time." He will not tell me when my time comes because he has given me plenty of prep time. If I fail in this preparation period called life, I'm in big trouble. This place of preparation moves in only one direction, forward. I can't go back. My life is irreversible just as time is.

If a scientist were to ask me if time has a beginning, my answer will always be God is the Alpha and the Omega. My life's journey has been determined by the forward movement of time he provides. This is the reason looking backwards doesn't change my forward movement. But looking backwards is turning my face from God. He has already told me to look to the future. A future with him is my time-measured goal. I need a clock to measure my existence on earth, but after my life ends I won't have to worry about Albert Einstein's Theory of Relativity that attempted to define time.

May God give all of us time to prepare as we travel through life without looking back but looking forward to our final home. I am a soldier marching forward to the tick-tock of time, marching toward my permanent home. I only hope the gates of heaven will open for my entry.

Are We Ready?

When God calls us, will we be ready to stand before him? Well, it doesn't really make a difference if we are ready or not since God is the Great Decision Maker. He makes decisions about us and for us. As Christians we know there will be his Second Coming. Revelation 22:12 is a verse we should remember. **"Behold, I am coming soon! My reward is with me, and I will give to everyone according to what they have done."** Do we believe this? We should because Jesus has never told an untruth. Jesus made it clear only the Father really knows the time of the Second Coming. Jesus knows he will come only as the Father determines. He knows if we knew the date and time we would only get ready just before the day rather than preparing ourselves throughout life. We worry about the unimportance and forget about Judgement Day.

Revelation states when Jesus comes, he will separate the goats from the sheep. The goats are those who did nothing for his fellow man. The sheep are those who offered help and were generous to others. Jesus could have spoken of other domesticated animals of his time: cattle, chickens, and camels, but he referred to sheep to teach lessons. Sheep band together for protection. If one moves in a certain direction, the others will follow. Jesus wants us to band together and protect each other from danger and the evil one. Sheep run from danger and when there is a shepherd, they move toward him. They are comforted by him and stand close together for a visual link to each other.

We must believe we will be judged one day. We need to learn from sheep what Jesus wants from us. We should band together for his protection and assist others to become part of his mighty flock. The final lesson is to keep our eyes on the true prize, eternal life. When Jesus comes, the Great Decision Maker will determine the day and the time, and we need to be ready. We should try to make daily preparations for our readiness, hoping he will accept us into his heaven, our final home.

Did You Hear Him or See Him?

It is so hard to pray without wondering if our prayers will be answered. We are so used to the visibility of this world we can seldom release what we see, feel and hear while we pray. The most difficult thing that happens is that the five senses seem to be obstacles. We pray with tears in our eyes, we are begging for forgiveness, we are shouting out our need for help. We may be prostrate on the floor or kneeling with our hands folded and our eyes toward heaven. We can't see God standing in a flowing white robe telling us that our prayers have been answered. We can't send an email expecting a return message telling us the message has been received and our problems will be resolved in 24 hours. I think our faith would be stronger if we could see and hear him.

We all pray everyday by saying thanks for being visibly a part of this physical world. We don't know what the spiritual world will provide for us. It is a mystery we have not been able to solve. We think we will be alone without anyone to care for us. So we keep praying and begging, praying and begging because we are uncertain. God will answer our prayers. We keep crying with the same message over and over again. If God is so powerful why do we think he can't hear or speak? Our parents heard us when we asked, cried and begged for things. Why don't you think God hears us as we pray since he is our heavenly **Father**?

God has an ineffable record for keeping his promises. The Bible details his promises and if we believe we will hear his voice in our consciousness, and we will see him in what we reap for following his path. Our goal is to get to his house and not to your neighbor's house. There is no mystery in his words. He has told us how to reach his domain. His address and telephone number is prayer and when the letters are dialed it is 447-9673. We have always been able to see and hear him. Now is this physical enough for you?

Death Is New Life

We have seen the passing of friends and relatives into eternal life. We cannot begin to know the happiness they must feel being in God's presence. His promises to them were revealed and honored. We usually say that we are among the living, but I believe those that have passed into God's realm are the true living. There is no pain or worries about mortgages or rent. No pain or worry about whether the changing seasons will bring new challenges. They have made it into the Promised Land being assured there is a God.

As we are formed in our mother's womb there are only two things we must face: life and death. Being born into this world is a time of preparation in which you can make choices for good or evil. We are given time to make this thing called life work for us. We never know the time or place when he will call us to his side, and we want to hear the words, "Well done, my child."

Those of us who are on this side of death are afraid of a robed skeleton carrying a sickle, yet not realizing God would not want to send this image as a collector of life. I believe he would only send an angel of beauty who has always been with us to tell us it is time to travel a new journey. We don't understand what we will face. We only understand people familiar to us. This is the renting status of this world. When the lease expires people move to a better place that doesn't require payment for time or space. Our leases are written in the words of God.

There should be a celebration when one passes because all pain and worry has ended for them. Our memories are reminders we are still loved by them and our Lord and Master. These memories should be a guide to our preparation period on this earth. Eulogies are a history of how our loved ones tried to get this thing called life **right**. If the words of the eulogies are true, be aware that a roadmap to the Lord has been left for us by these time travelers. The word of God is also our roadmap to salvation. Don't lean on the Word, stand on it. These roadmaps are our individual plans to reach the Redeemer. He's waiting with open arms and will judge the success of our travels to him.

I Know Him

Throughout my life I have seen tragedy and
pain, yet my God saw me through.

As I walked in faith, God gave me strength
to endure with angels at my side.

Some angels were invisible and some were
visible to guide me on my journey.

The Holy Spirit spoke to me often to give me
the messages God sent through him.

So many people have been good to me as I look
forward to going home to see the Lord.

When I hear the voice of the Holy Spirit it has
always been with a comforting softness.

All the time I have known I am in God's hands and
he makes the final decision about my life.

I thank God for everything he has done for me and
the love I received from family and friends.

What Is the Body of Christ?

I wonder if we as Christians truly understand the meaning of "The Body of Christ". Do we sometimes consider it to be a social club? There are momentous differences between being a member of the Body of Christ and a member of a social club. A social club requires a member to meet at a specific time and day. They come together to laugh, share the same interests, and to emphasize what it is designed to do. Members go home, live their lives, come back, and do the same thing again. Usually, there are dues to be paid to maintain the exclusive membership. Sometimes in life we have belonged to some type of club, for example, a fraternity, sorority, bridge club, dance club, or reading club. Were you ever a dependable member or an officer with authority? What duties did you perform to ensure you fit into the model membership? Just pause and think about the latter questions for a moment, then compare them to the Body of Christ.

When we talk about the body of a car usually we are not referring to the engine, wheels and other parts that cause the car to operate. We are only interested in the exterior looks, then later we want to test-drive. Sometimes we do the same with our faith. We look at the superficial then the manageable parts and only do a test drive. In St. Paul's first letter to the Corinthians in Chapter 12: 12-31 he provides a vivid description of how the whole is represented the parts of the body. Each part works on behalf of the other parts. His usage of the body as an image is telling us that Jesus is the whole and we are his related parts. The members of Christ's body come together to worship and glorify God. We come to church just as we would go to a hospital. We are going to be revived and strengthened. We pay no dues for this membership because his death was payment for all our debts. We owe no fines or penalties. Our free-will of love for God is payment enough for him. He does not exclude anyone and his expectations are always the same: love and obey based on his teachings.

We are not expected to be officers who decide the fate and actions of others, but participants of love and evangelizing in his behalf. There is no time schedule for us to become part of this Body. In this Body we don't have to look a certain way, dress a certain way, or be denied membership for any reason. The caveat to this membership is there are three persons who love, guide, and protect us 24/7. Do you get this in a social club? There is nothing wrong with membership in social clubs, but the foremost membership is in the Body of Christ.

"Whom Shall I Fear"

The first verse of Psalm 27 has an important question for all of us. The question has to do with fear in our lives.

"The Lord is my light and my salvation; whom shall I fear? The Lord is the strength of my life; of whom shall I be afraid?"

We have fears that result from a weak or lack of faith in the Master who created us. Situations in life cause us to fear what seem unsurmountable problems. We think we can control a situation and find the situation is controlling us. We fear losing a job, fear losing a house to foreclosure, fear losing a so-called loving relationship, fear death, fear of family problems and just plain "ole" fear. Psalm 27 tells us we don't have to fear worldly challenges because God will fight our battles. Our minds light up when we have prayed and God has given us an answer. His answer is knowledge that lights up our minds to change our attitude toward the situation. We then begin to see how to solve the problems letting God be our guide. Our salvation is our deliverance or our rescue from all harm when God changes our attitudes with clarity. The clarity is to **"Let go and let God."**

God gives us the strength to go through the challenges of life. An old saying, **"If God brings you to it, he will bring you through it."** He gives us the strength to give our enemies a "knockout punch" at his hands. His muscles are our muscles; His love is our love that defeats the enemies swiftly and permanently. Sometimes we are so sure we can handle a problem we swell up like a toad only to be devoured by a predator who has been lying in wait. Psalms 56:11 says, **"In God I put my trust; I will not be afraid. What can man do to me?"** Man can try to do a bunch to us, but if we wait patiently on God's muscle in the boxing ring of life, we can hold up our arms as winners. With God's muscle the enemy goes down for the count. Not the count of ten, but the count of one.

We are always going to have fears that grit our nerves, but what we forget is the battle garb of God. Put on the belt of truth. Be truthful in our endeavors and with others. Put on the breastplate of righteousness. Justice is what we are looking for while being as blameless as we can be. Stand on the gospel of peace because violence gains nothing. Wear the shield of faith. Believe God can do all things though we don't see him; he is with us for true victory. Put on the helmet of salvation. Know the mercy of God is the greatest gift to all mankind. Encase the sword of the Spirit of the Word. Read and understand the New Testament compliments the Old Testament. Note, these parts of our battle garb are not as heavy as the apparel of the knights of the Middle Ages. We can always carry them. Remember, Psalms 4:3 **"The Lord will hear when I call."** Believe! Believe! Believe!

II

TROUBLES

What's Your Cross?

I want you to take a minute and think about the question above before you continue to read. How long have you been carrying this cross? Is the cross a result of something in your past or in your present? Now, I want you to examine your innermost thoughts. Remember, no one knows this cross you bear. It's been veiled. So you think. But others can tell you have a heavy burden because you have allowed the burden to define who you are. Some people carry their burdens with a smile. Others carry them with anger. Anger is revealing. For those who carry the burden with a smile, the burden has gotten lighter over time because they have surrendered themselves to God. He began to lighten the load and take it away with revelation and understanding. Those who carry the load with anger have not released the burden to the mighty Problem Solver.

We all question why we are having unsolvable problems. We act as if we are SuperMan by making a quick change in a closet and flying through the air as fast as the speed of light. Go sit yourself down and come back to reality. We look at others and question why them? They seem to be without problems. Everything is "hunky dory" with them. Yet, you are sinking in quicksand up to your chin. You're in a state of confusion. You can't move your body. You're screaming for help. But you're screaming for the wrong person to help you. There is a person in heaven waiting for you to call his name and he will be the one who comes as fast as the speed of light. What? How? Wow! No more burden.

You called his name. JESUS.

Issues

Everyone of us faces personal issues. They may be family issues, health issues, financial issues, legal issues, and family deaths, but whatever the issues may be we have to face them. These are the challenges of life that God helps us through if we ask. Sometimes we forget what the Bible tells us. It says if we ask, we shall receive. If we knock, the door will be open. If we seek, we shall find. We should hold these words close to our hearts. Ask, seek, knock are three words that indicate a powerful relationship with our Father. Because he is our Father, his advice is always foolproof. He makes no errors leading us away from all temptations and all evil.

We have a tendency to think we can handle any problems that come to us. We think we have answers with a wisdom no one else has. Then all of a sudden the problem has become more difficult. We suddenly cannot find a solution. The problem has become a calculus problem and since we were not math majors we have no solution. This is the time we drop to our knees and ask for help from the Father. Hands clasped, knees bent, and tears pouring like a rainstorm. This is when we are forced to admit we don"t have answers. We didn't even have the power to get rid of those involved in the problem. Here we go again thinking we're the Wizard.

When we dropped to our knees and prayed to the real Wizard, we finally realized God is our wizard. We realize if we ask, he gives, when we knock at his door we are welcomed, when we seek, he provides all the answers. He understands our stupidity with mercy. Before an issue becomes a daunting problem go to the Master first. As the gospel song says **"He may not come when you want him, but he'll be there right on time. He's an on time God, yes he is."**

Here Comes the Pity Party

Have you ever sat on the side of your bed or on a chair with tears streaming down your face? You're trying to hold back the tears, but they seem to roll down your face like an open facet. Feeling sorry for yourself is only an indication things have not gone your way. As tears fall you question your self-worth. Am I pretty enough? Where is the money I need to pay my bills? My employer questions my ability to remain on the job. I can't seem to achieve my goals. There are so many reasons why you devalue yourself as a person. But there is a short Jewish saying that is a reminder it could be worse: "I felt sorry for myself because I had no shoes. Then I met a man who had no feet." We all get down in the dumps sometimes forgetting the many blessings we have had and how many will come. This emotion is a human frailty that can be overcome.

Everyone should have an earthly friend whom you can talk to. I have prayer partners who are friends and when they pray, watch out! Between the three of us answers come and the blessings pour down like the self-pitying tears of the open facet. We can cry together, pray together, protect each other, and tell each other when one of us is wrong, yet love each other. Our lips are zipped when personal problems occur because we know our Heavenly Warrior is on the job. My earthly prayer partners and I can testify how good God is. I can't ever forget my Master who probably says, "Connie, Julia, and Joann are calling again."

Learning to accept the obstacles placed before us reminds us to get on our knees then stand tall because a prayer partner is with us. The earthly prayer partners have been on their knees and stand tall when you face adversity and during good times. Stand up, head held high, and stand still and let God fix it. God has got your back. There is nothing like prayer partners. Find yours and hold on to them as they hold on to you for similar support. No more pity parties, but just know God never devalues his children. If you know you are a child of God pull the shades up and let the sunshine in. The warmth of the sun is the same warmth you will feel as God wraps his arms around you. Pity those who don't know him.

Our Storms

In 2017 we have heard and seen the devastation of Hurricane Harvey and Hurricane Irma. Weathermen report there is another hurricane developing in the Atlantic Ocean. It appears there is one storm after another. These hurricanes have brought death and destruction to people and property. People feel helpless and empty as they wait for help. Meteorologists rate hurricanes by categories one, two, three four and five. The fifth category being the worst with winds of one hundred ninety miles per hour. As we journey through life, just think how we might compare our personal storms with the hurricane categories.

When I had to divorce my husband, this was my category 5. It hurt so much that I often wondered could I have done more to hold the marriage together. My choice was to end it and I never married again. We all have our storms based on fear, unhappiness, helplessness, being unloved, or being homeless physically and spiritually. One thing we have learned as Christians is to have faith in our Lord and Master who brings us through all the storms we face. It seems as if our lives have been a portrayal of day-by-day struggles. One of the most important struggles is being a true Christian. We keep wondering if there will be a place for us in heaven. This is when we should be more worried we have not said, "Sorry, Lord." Asking for forgiveness and mercy will help acquire that place in eternity.

In Mark 4:36-41 we are reminded of the power of Jesus, the Son of God. Jesus was tired and laid his head on a cushion in a boat with the apostles. A storm developed on the Sea of Galilee causing high winds that caused high level winds to rush water into the boat. Four of the disciples were fishermen and I'm sure they had seen these storms before but they were all afraid this time. They shouted "Teacher, don't you care if we drown?" Jesus stretched out his arm and said, "Quiet! Be still." If we have faith Jesus will quiet our storms. Don't let the hurricane categories determine your fate. Your fate is in the hands of Jesus our God. He remarked, "Why are you terrified? Do you not have faith?" This remark describes many of us.

Our faith seems to dwindle when we are entering a storm. As the storm increases and it weighs down on us, we finally ask God for help. If we had faith to begin with, the storm would not have gained strength. When Jesus muzzled the storm the disciples asked who was this man who could quiet a storm? They didn't know at the time and that's why they called him "Teacher". It took them time. It takes us time if we are not reading Scripture. Reading and understanding gives us the armor to fight evil and win. When the showers of life come, lighting cracks as our mind and hearts quake, and thunder rebounds around us as a heavy weight. This is our category one. This tells us to reach out to Jesus and let Him calm the storm before it becomes a category five.

Sometimes, Lord

Fifteen or twenty years ago, while I was feeling lonely and depressed I wrote this poem. Writing this poem was my way of releasing the down spirit I felt and it brought me back to the reality of my God. I said what I wanted to say to God and this was therapeutic for me. Sometimes when you are in a low spirit write down how you feel. In the meantime, I will share these words with you.

Sometimes, Lord

Sometimes Lord, I wish I could see your face.
Wondering how you look is only a part of my imagination.
Most people in this country picture you as white,
But Lord, I see you as me.

Sometimes Lord, I wish there was a response to my questions.
I talk and don't hear a voice with answers for my prying mind.
When I'm very quiet in a quiet place I tend to hear you.
Suddenly, I hear you in this silence when my
soul becomes a radio receiver.

Sometimes Lord, my prayers don't seem to be heard.
It appears you're taking a vacation.
Usually, you're on vacation when I pray for material things.
You seem to know what I need instead of what I want.

Sometimes Lord, I just need you to say loudly "Everything is okay.
Be patient my daughter and just wait. I will provide all your needs."
Lord, my faith is a little shaky at times,
But, if I can't see you I can feel your presence that strengthens me.

Sometimes Lord, I need to say thank you for the gifts you have given me.
I should not forget what you'll give me in the future.
These gifts will lead to the greatest of all gifts, eternal life with you.
See Lord, I try to live by your holy words as the Holy Spirit guides me.
Forgive me for my weaknesses, Lord.
Thank you, Lord, for listening.

A Spiritual Reflection

Every day brings a new experience. A person may have spoken harsh words to you. A new pain arose to make you wonder what is happening to your body. Your finances are in a shambles. However, you may remember a Sunday sermon that encouraged you or gave you strength. Maybe you reached for your Bible searching for inspiring words to bring you peace. Maybe the words of a song remind you of something so personal it brought tears to your eyes. Have you ever thought how blessed you are to be able to hear words, to feel pain, to have shambled finances, to still have a memory? How wonderful it is to awaken every morning to have these experiences.

The latter reminds us we are trees that stand for years enduring storms and droughts. But we know each season may bring hardships that strip some of the bark from our trunks. We know leaves may turn vibrant colors for one season and for another season drop to the ground. But the deep strong roots hold us securely. Sometimes lightning may strike us, but our roots remain deep in the bosom of rich soil. No matter what we go through we have spiritual support in the Lord Jesus Christ who carries us through and over every obstacle. Welcome hard times because they allow us to know we are alive and "kickin". Welcome obstacles because we grow in faith just as trees find ways to survive during hard times.

To me, this is the meaning of the resurrection of Jesus and proves we have strong roots. Our roots are stronger since we hold tightly to our faith. We are as strong as a tree. Each season is our spiritual resurrection. This is our awakening of a great sacrifice made by someone who loves us. We now have a guarantee of eternal life. As the tree stays fixed in one space the seeds travel to share the beauty and strength of the parent tree and it always reaches upward to praise and be thankful for the sacrifice.

III

WHAT MATTERS

God's Breath

We inhale and exhale twelve to eighteen times per minute. While we are asleep and when awake there is continuous breathing that sends oxygen through our bodies while carbon dioxide is released. Carbon dioxide is a poisonous gas we exhale but it is not wasted. Plants use this gas to make their food. Have you ever thought how our breath is the breath of God? He shares his breath to remind us our bodies are working at full capacity. We assume our bodies work automatically without assistance. Well, it needs oxygen supplied by someone who is constantly giving us air to breathe.

God is such a Giver of Life that every function of our bodies is dependent on him. One organ that needs oxygen is the brain. It maintains a mind full of ideas and thoughts. Ideas cause us to invent, discover, and preserve. Thoughts give us circumspection to meditate on our Creator and our souls. Our souls are within us, though we do not know its specific location. God said he would always be with us just as our souls would be.

Look at your surroundings as you breathe. Have you taken your surroundings for granted just as you have taken the ability to breathe for granted? God has given us three ways to breathe: through the nose, the skin, and the mouth. He gives our lungs the diligent responsibility of transporting oxygen throughout our bloodstreams so the twelve to eighteen breaths per minute perpetuate life. God gives us so much we take for granted. Our ability to breathe is God's mechanized system to support life. He works on our behalf 24/7 with compassion and love. Take a deep breath today while saying, "Thank you, God." Hold it! Release. Does that breath remind you of God's goodness or will you remain ignorant of his powers?

The Mouth

I remember asking my grandmother why God made our faces like they were. I had been reading science fiction stories where the creatures had faces with three eyes, no mouth, and their ears on top of their heads while living on other planets. I kind of believed at the time, there would be life on other planets. (Still do) My imagination would go wild reading the short stories and books. My grandmother succinctly answered that God gave us one mouth to speak less, two ears to listen more, and two eyes to see God's wonderful world. I don't know if she read this somewhere or if it was something she felt in her heart. Sometimes she would tell me to close my mouth when I was a child because I was talking too much. Through the years I have understood what powerful advice she had given me in her statement.

The mouth allows air and nutrients to enter our bodies to bring health and strength for our bodies to function. We have also learned that words have energy and power with the ability to hurt, heal, humiliate, hinder, help or harm as they escape the mouth. It depends on what words we allow to escape. The Bible mentions the mouth 424 times making us aware how words can affect us and others. We can praise or curse depending on the intent of our words. One quote says " What is in man's heart comes out of his mouth." Sometimes we need to ask ourselves if our words are sour or sweet. If our words are meant to hurt or heal. Sometimes we just need to keep our mouths shut because we don't know the impact of our spoken words.

Jealousy and envy cause intentional hurt. But how gentle and inspiring were the words of Jesus and his Father. No jealousy or envy, just messages of love and understanding. His father gave us his only Son as the final covenant of mercy for us. Our words should never defile ourselves or others. Say them always with the energy of God's love. Granny may still be saying, "Girl, you're still talking too much." That's why I write.

The Mouth and Words

God created a human body that is perfect in every way. The mouth is the most interesting to me because it is the cavity for ingestion, digestion, and creating speech by using the tongue, teeth, and lips. From the mouth comes the ability to express thoughts and feelings by articulating sounds understood by others. When we digest food, all the cells in the body benefit from the intake. Ten thousand taste buds on the tongue allow us to determine if we are ingesting something sweet, sour, bitter, or salty. Words from our mouths should benefit our minds with positive thoughts and ideas just as ingestion of food benefits the body. Our words skim over our taste buds while determining if the words will be sweet, sour, bitter, or salty. God says the tongue has incredible power. It can be used to bring blessings and life, or curses and death.

The Bible makes reference to the mouth 87 times. Proverbs 15:4 says, a tree **"The soothing tongue is a tree of life, but a perverse tongue crushes the spirits."** Psalm 34:13 states **"Those who guard the mouths, and their tongues keep themselves from calamity."** Guarding our words in all situations permits the mind to determine if the words need to be said. They can activate a negative behavior from one receiving the words, or can inspire thoughts for creativity and improve behavior. Words roll over the taste buds for good or evil.

We are all guilty of sometimes saying the wrong thing at the wrong time and then wish we had not said them. We may shout at our children or spouse when a softer voice may have accomplished the same objective. Gossiping about someone is usually based on jealousy or just a plain evil intent that is meant to hurt. The gossiper finds it easy to tell a lie about someone because of their own shortcomings.

If we practice the teaching of Jesus, we notice his voice always seemed calm in the reading of the Bible. We have to open our mouths to encourage thoughts Jesus expressed in words and deeds. Kind words heal the spirit and make a smile indicate thanks or relief from pain. Kind words have a positive reaction for the receiver, and the giver benefits, too. When we open our mouths to receive the Holy Eucharist, we don't want a residue of evil to be inside our mouths nor do we want to exit the church ready to gossip. Gossip is garbage that leaves a residue of nastiness on the teeth and tongue. The teeth need brushing and the mouth requires an antiseptic.

Words have power for good or for evil. When we open this cavity, make sure it is not contaminated with evil. The taste buds will let you know if the words are sweet, sour, bitter, or salty because they are 10,000 strong. They are the receptors that determine the flavor of each word. They reveal who we are as they roll over the 10,000 taste buds. Let's watch our word. Let words be drenched with kindness.

A Wonderful Gift

God has given us all a wonderful gift that is the most important and complex organ of the body. It has an unlimited storage capacity and weighs about three pounds. It is more active at night than during the day. Information travels within this organ at a speed of about 265 miles per hour for storage from our visuals that become memories. We have a tendency to think this organ can feel pain, but the muscles and skin near it cause the pain. God has given us this gift that allows us to control our thoughts, memories, speech, and body movements of our arms and legs. This organ is the brain.

Take a look back and remember the scarecrow in the *Wizard of Oz* searching for a brain. He wanted one so badly. We have been gifted with one.

Everyday God has given us the ability to see and learn about ourselves and others. These created memories are stored for coordination of our actions and reactions, allowing us to think, concentrate, and feel. When reading the Bible, the words should cause us to think, concentrate for meaning and understanding. It causes our brain to react to these words for an active belief in God's love and power. We speak of his words through our actions and reactions. They are the stored pictures we need to always spread the Word of God. As Timothy 3:16 states " All Scripture is breathed out by God and profitable for teaching."

We may be living in a time of chaos, but our brain helps us to make decisions that are unselfish and loving. God's love gives us free will to decide if we will follow him to the road to righteousness or to the road of emptiness and darkness. Our thoughts are our ideas,opinions and beliefs that should always lead us to the one who made us.The beauty of having a brain is we can do nothing without it. This is the same for our God. **<u>We can do nothing without Him.</u>**

A Road that Matters

No one ever told me the road to maturity and the road to God would be easy. Here I am, 82 years old and still trying to stay on the pathway that leads to eternal life. St. Paul has always intrigued me with his unyielding words of faith to the Jews and the Gentiles. He walked, talked and sailed throughout the Middle East to spread the news of a man who gave us redemption and eternal life. Even with the sacrifice Jesus made for us, the road to our Savior is still packed with obstacles. Sometimes I feel I'm at the bottom of a steep mountain looking up and asking myself can I really make it to the pinnacle of this mountain. Then I will have to come down again. If I make it, another hurdle appears.

Sometimes I am so tired knowing I have to make another climb, but I just think of Jesus, St. Paul, and other biblical figures. They met obstacles, but I don't know if I am strong enough to overcome them alone. I do know that if I keep praying the mountains will become level plains. " I shall fear no evil." Jesus and St. Paul will see me through because my faith has ripened with my maturity. My faith is like my own home-grown fertilizer that causes one's life to be enriched with belief in a Savior. I am learning to follow his footprints and am aware he also pushes me forward. O my goodness, here's another mountain! Let me get a grip! Lord, have mercy, I feel him within me!

IV

IMAGERY

Expect Delays

One day I sat thinking how God answers prayer. Sometimes he's quick to answer and sometimes he takes a while. Sometimes he even substitutes other things than what we prayed for, yet, he always answers our prayers. This brought to my mind a traffic sign when there is road construction being done. Before you get to the construction site there is a sign about a half mile prior that says **EXPECT DELAYS.** As we get to the construction site, traffic is as slow as a turtle's pace. We get frustrated as we wait to again do the normal speed limit. When we finally get to the end of the construction we press the gas pedal to reach the normal speed limit or beyond the speed limit. Our minds are on getting to our destination.

I began to apply this traffic warning to how and when we expect God to answer our prayers. We seem to always expect immediate gratification from God instead of letting him do what he does best. He answers when he wants and when his answer is best for us. We beg, we cry, we get frustrated, and we even begin to believe we are not worthy of his help. We forget the words of a prayerful grandmother who says he is always on time. Scripture says "Everyone who asks, receives; the one who seeks will find; and the one who knocks, the door shall be opened." Our God keeps his promises.

Be patient because God knows what we need, why we need, and when we need. He is with us at all times. As the road construction improves the road surface and the lanes are widened, think how God allows improvements in our lives and widens our vision to see the things to come. With faith he always leads and directs us to our destinations.

Breakfast With A Celebrity

What would you do if Barack Obama's Office called you to have breakfast? Would you be speechless or tremble with nervousness? Or would you faint and drop to the floor? After accepting the invitation you probably would call all your friends and relatives to let them know President Obama has invited you to breakfast. You will be driven to the restaurant in a limousine. How elegant! The next thing you may consider is the outfit you will wear, or you may have to shop for a new one. Preparations, preparations, preparations! The excitement is overwhelming. Your hair! What about your hair? Oh my, you must look well groomed for this fantastic day. Wow! You just can't believe you had been chosen to have breakfast with him. This will be the greatest day of your life. It will be a memory to always remember.

Now the next question I will ask is what if God invited you to breakfast? Would you call all your friends and family? Would you be worried about what you would wear or how your hair looked? Would you be excited to know you had been invited by him? Instead of a limousine he's bringing everything to you. You will see him, face to face, just as President Obama would speak to you face to face. What things would you talk about with God since he knew you in your mother's womb? You have been asking him to provide you with a way to pay your bills, find a job, put food on your table, cure your illness, and so many other requests. You have sometimes turned your back on him who has provided so much. President Obama could only give you one day of pleasure, while God has given and will give you a lifetime of happiness.

Are you still thinking of what you would do if God invited you to breakfast? You have not considered he provides breakfast, lunch and dinner daily. He is your chief provider of all the things you enjoy as you journey through life. He has seen you at your worst and at your best. When you have challenges he brings you through them. What have you given him as you sit at his feast? Are you gobbling up all that's on his table and walk away without showing appreciation. President Obama isn't able to provide for you because he depends on the goodness and mercy from God, also. God knew him in his mother's womb. Each day of life should be your celebration for God's gifts. Remember, God has given you so much. How much have you given him? I hope I have given you something to think about in this writing. You should want a lifetime membership in TYLC (Thank You Lord Club). It's the banking club that pays dividends for your membership.

Cruising With the Holy Spirit

I once had a job I didn't like. Each day was always a necessary challenge for me. People and situations arose that had jealousy and injustice standing like a brick wall before me. Yet, I kept saying thank you Lord for another day that I breathe and another day for the chance to change what I can change with your help.

I always believe God puts us in a certain place, at a specific time, for a specific reason, and as I wrote this I understood God's lesson for me. The job was given to me to help others and I was doing this as an " old retired war horse". I found myself tired of giving and I had sometimes ignored my own needs. Everybody seemed to want something from me and I often felt drained. I wanted to come home, close the door and not speak to a single soul. I wanted to lie on my bed and read the three books a week I usually read. I wanted to have time to write the book I had been trying to write for five years with chapters written and rewritten. I was tired all the time. I felt like the actress Greta Garbo who said this famous statement: "I want to be alone." Maybe in my efforts to help others I was doing too much, but there were so many in need. Finally, I said to myself that I was going to let the Holy Spirit guide me while I sat in the back seat and allowed him to drive in the best direction for me.

During this time of anguish, I received a Christmas gift from my Bible Buddy, Anita Herring, and it took me a week or two before I started reading it. The book is entitled <u>The Transforming Word </u> by Tony Evans. The author writes that the words of the Bible should cause a transformation within the individual who takes time to read it. Well, I thought of my job as a sour lemon. Maybe it could turn into lemonade if I released my negative emotions. Through the gift of a book I was revitalized and ready to cruise with the Holy Spirit.

As the Holy Spirit and I were cruising down the road, the first traffic sign read **Confusion Road**. Confusion was a wrong detour for me and I believed I would have taken this road if the Holy Spirit had not been with me. I am the nosy kind and would have been in a deep mess if this road was traveled.The next sign was **Go For It**. It was a wide boulevard and this is where we decided to rest. We chatted about my planning and organizational strategies needed for this job. The waitress who approached us was an angel offering the best ideas on the menu which were sustenances. As we returned to our chariot of justice there was a smile on my face. There was peace and joy that beheld me. When cruising with the Holy Spirit there were no traffic accidents to deter us from our destination. I do have the road atlas for a reference, the Bible. I don't want the Holy Spirit to get a traffic violation because of me. Riding in the chariot of justice with well eaten nourishment changed me. Guess what! The job became lemonade and people became kinder.

Getting Rid of Junk

There are all types of commercials on television, but one that struck my attention was the commercial that tells people they can get rid of junk. The person who called to remove their junk only had to snap their finger and the junk was gone. The reason it caught my attention was because it was during Lent. This was the season to rid ourselves of the spiritual junk we carry and to remember the faithfulness of God. God gave us his Son to be sacrificed for the many sins of man. On the cross, Jesus, through all his torture, still asked for forgiveness for those who denied his teachings. Could we have done what he did for us? Think about that.

During the season of Lent we are reminded to rid ourselves of the junk we carry in our hearts and minds. We have allowed our mouths to make sinners of us. We have made promises we did not intend to keep. When a wrong or evil thought comes to mind we have had two choices: entertain the thought or refuse to act. These thoughts are junk needing to go to the garbage dump. If we call ourselves Christians do we focus on encouraging and comforting others or are we too busy, have too much to do, or just don't care about anyone else? This is junk that needs to go to the garbage dump or recycled for better use

When our mouths spurt out gossip that can hurt someone's reputation or cause them mental stress, it gives truthfulness no way to recover. The enemies of Jesus ridiculed him with untruths because they would forfeit power and depreciate favor among the Romans. We can't be afraid of the truth. It is beneficial to all. It allows justice and equity to flourish. Denying truth is junk that causes heartaches that damage a person's very soul.

This commercial can cause us to think about our own junk that needs to go to the garbage heap. We need to think if we can recycle (ask forgiveness) our junk. Prayer helps us refuse to act on evil thoughts and speak words of unkindness. God has a truck that removes all junk. The truck's name is The **Prayer Line**. Never busy and removes junk quickly..

Guided Travels

While sitting in front of my computer my thoughts turned to the Underground Railroad. The thought of fleeing slaves traveling to freedom and wondering what was ahead of them. They traveled through unknown territory and in all kinds of weather. What brought this on I can't tell you except that the thought was there. Some of the runaway slaves died on their journey. Harriet Tubman led seventy people to freedom. She made thirteen trips for others to win their freedom. There were twenty miles between each station (safe house). Rail agents were available every 20 miles to take the runaways to a safe house. When the runaways left one safe house other agents would take them another twenty miles to another safe house. Harriet Tubman usually traveled the entire route until the freedom destination was reached. The state of Illinois and 25 other states had other routes to bring the runaways to freedom traveling hundreds and sometimes thousands of miles. Suddenly, I thought about Mary and Joseph and questioned how I could relate their travels to the Underground Railroad.

Mary and Joseph were forced to leave their home in Nazareth, and travel to Bethlehem. *"In those days Caesar Augustus issued a decree that a census must be taken of the entire Roman world. Everyone went to his own town to register. So, Joseph also went up from the town of Nazareth in Galilee to Judea, to Bethlehem the town of David, because he belonged to the house and line of David. He went there to register with Mary, who had pledged to be married to him and was expecting a child." (Luke 2:1-5)*. This journey probably took them about four to seven days to travel 80 miles to Bethlehem. They traveled in all kinds of weather and over unknown terrain. God was their agent guiding them as they traveled from one point to another. When they arrived in Bethlehem the stable was their safe house. God had been their Harriet Tubman. Forty days after the birth of Jesus, Mary and Joseph traveled 6 miles to the temple in Bethlehem. They followed the Jewish law of presenting a child to God. This was another safe house because the Romans allowed the Jews to practice their religion in their temples.

Joseph was told by his Station Master (his God) to leave Bethlehem and take his family to Egypt. Crazy Herod was killing all the male children two years of age and younger in Bethlehem. It was a 40-mile trip through the controlled territory of the Romans. The country of Egypt was their safe house. Then after their stayed in Egypt there was a 160-mile trek back to Nazareth. God was with them all the way as they traveled to a place of freedom to protect the child, Jesus. It seems they traveled about 290 miles from one place to another. Again, God was their spiritual Harriet Tubman.

Think about the mileage in our lives. Each day the Station Master has led us to safe houses to fulfill our missions in life. We may not be a heroine like Harriet Tubman or a warrior like Dr. Martin Luther King Jr. but think of the many journeys of life we have traveled to our freedom of mind, body, and spirit. God defied the powers of the Romans. Harriet Tubman defied the law of slavery and never lost an Underground Railroad passenger as God never denies protection for his sheep. **Mission accomplished!** Did you enter a safe house recently? When you travel the road of life, the doors of freedom and forgiveness will open. The Station Master will guide you to the final safe house, Heaven.

A Question of Image

As Christians, do we ever question the true meaning of how "God created man in his own image…"? Do we understand what the image of God is? This question came to my mind as I prayed my daily prayers. My physical image of God is based on the cultural pictures I have seen, but my physical and personal image is of a black man. Is this image really important? God's son walked the earth to sacrifice himself for us. He hung with excruciating pain while asking forgiveness for those who wronged him. Yet, God created even those who mistreated his Son. Did those who disrespected his Son ever know the physical features of God? They probably would have been shocked. Even Moses was shocked as he saw the image of God as a burning bush but not his face.

When we say we are created in God's image, his physical features are not what the statement actually means. We have to look deeper to understand the spiritual features he has given us. He gave us free will to choose to make the choices to follow, love, and obey him just as Jesus did for his father. He forgives all of us over and over again. He is merciful at all times. He loves all his people even when they turn away from him. His only desire is for us to model our lives after his spiritual goodness so salvation is available to us.

Let's end our interest in God's physical image since he created us in his spiritual image of positive attributes. Our journey through life is dependent on the images we portray to him and to others. It's not how we look, nor what we have, or what we know. It depends on how close we want to be to God and imitate his spiritual goodness. When we meet people let's look for the image of God within them and expose his spiritual greatness within us to them. He said we were created in his image, **so let it be.**

Are You Ready For Battle?

I have been reminded by the words of a friend that there is a need to be prepared for battle with the devil who works daily to gain souls for his realm. I thought about this and decided to read the Scripture to determine my readiness for the daily struggles I will encounter. Sometimes, I get weak during the day and almost want to give up. I say to myself "Why me?" and the inner voice says with firmness rsponds "Why not you?" To the Scriptures I ran to totally define getting ready for these battles.

In Ephesians Chapter 6:10-20 there is a strong message on how to fight evil. The first step is to wrap ourselves in truth, head to toe. Know that the words of Scripture are God's truth then admit the truth about ourselves to God. Wear truth like we wear our personal clothing closest to our bodies. This is the first layer of armor necessary for protection.

Secondly, we must wear righteousness as our breast plate. This breast plate protects our hearts and our moral goodness from being corrupted by evil. It is the layer similar to our outer layer of clothing. Looking good, feeling good, and smelling good. This is the layer that others notice and will want to replicate.

Thirdly, we walk in peace wearing shoes that fit well and shine as radiantly as the sun. Peace is within us and we transfer this peace to others in deeds and in words. God wants us to have the inner peace to signal to others that our love of God gives us peace. All of us are children of God who can find the peacefulness in ourselves and in others whom we love and sometimes even offend. We walk in peace.

Fourthly, hold on to the faith we have that God is our Lord and we have been redeemed by the blood of his son, Jesus. Faith is the layer of protection that reminds us of a cloak or coat to protect us from the cold when the wind howls from an oncoming storm. If the wind is too strong we head for shelter and the shelter is the Lord. He puts his arms around us to renew our faith. So we hold on to our warm cloaks of faith.

Fifth, put on the helmet of salvation that protects the brain and mind from thoughts that hinder our route to heaven. Soldiers wear helmets in battle to protect injuries to the head. We are reminded that salvation is ours because we were rescued from sin and damnation. By the death of Jesus we have eternal life. Baptism assures us we have been given a reprieve from evil if we obey God's commands.Our mind and thoughts will continually be on the Master.

Sixth, pick up the sword that is the word of God. In other words, pick up our Bibles that are the weapons against evil. An armed soldier has to carry a weapon and the Bible is our weapon. The more we read, understand and practice the word we travel toward victory. God is with us in battle only if we are willing to use his weapon, then the battle is not ours alone, but the Lord's.

Let's get dressed for war! To the battlefield with our weapon! Lock and Load! Pow! Pow! Pow!

Having a Nightmare

Have you ever awakened in the middle of the night because of a bad dream? The dream scares you so much you must turn on your beside light and are too afraid to return to sleep. We all have had bad dreams in our lifetime that made us think of incidents that were real. Well, we know there were biblical prophets that had visions. For example, Jacob saw a ladder on earth that extended to heaven and the Lord was at the top. Another example is John having a vision of five beasts. But the one prophet Ezekiel, had one of the scariest dreams. His vision was a nightmare to me. He saw four humans with four faces and four wings. The four faces pointing in four different directions were the faces of a human, a face of a lion, a face of an ox, and a face of an eagle with each having two sets of wings. This is one of the weirdest visions I have read about.

As we read our Bibles there are lessons to be learned. Even while reading the Book of Ezekiel and doing a little research I began to understand the power and generosity of God. Visions were a way of communicating with individuals to get a message about God's plans. The prophets were chosen to help and warn the Israelites. They continue to be warnings even today.

We celebrate Thanksgiving, but do we celebrate our thanksgivings to God? He is the one who cares and protects us when we are afraid. We need to celebrate even the trials and tribulations that are our nightmares as we go through the day. We need to celebrate the life of friends and relatives who are only on loan to us as we are on loan to them. It is important to always be in a preparation mode for the coming of Christ Jesus. Just as our cell phones allow us to communicate with others. Our communication with God does not cost a single penny and it never needs batteries or an electrical cord to charge it. There is always a line to him while the Holy Spirit ensures our communication is always on a private line.

The four faces of the creatures Ezekiel saw were the splendor of our God.

The face of the man represents his gift of intelligence and understanding he gave to us. The lion represents his sovereignty and supremacy over all visible and invisible things in our universe. The ox represents the burdens he carries for us and sacrifices of mercy he bestows upon us. Finally, the eagle represents the soaring power of his majesty. Let's be thankful and be prepared for his coming. Praise God we have time to prepare.

In My House

In my house when I awaken in the morning I am alone in a physical sense, but in a spiritual sense I have a companion who assures me another day.

In my house I can look any way I want, and my companion accepts me when I look good, smell good, and feel good, or look beat down like a wet brown noodle.

In my house I can sit and read the latest news, yet my companion knows what was, what is, and what will be.

In my house I eat when I want and what I want, but my companion provides nourishment more than life itself.

In my house I may have a shut-off notice from the gas company, yet my companion will radiate warmth that sustains me.

In my house there may be no lights as I stumble into furniture, but my companion stretches out his hand to guide me through the darkness.

In my house when the telephone has no dial tone and I need to talk to someone, my companion has a 24 hour telephone line so I can communicate my thoughts and words to him.

When I visit his house I feel his presence, not because I say so, but because I know his essence.

When I visit his house he doesn't treat me like a guest, but like a member of his family.

Anytime I visit his house I can forget the troubles of the day, because he always has a commentary of peaceful joy.

In his house there is heat that sizzles more than the body.

In his house there is light that penetrates my very soul.

In his house I am his focus.

Did you notice he's the same in his house as he is in mine? He never changes.

Since we gather together in his house let's be awakened, nourished, and guided because we are one in him.

And when we leave his house, change. Try to be just like him. Love one another because my companion is my Mighty God.

The Master Contractor

Have you ever thought about how a contractor builds a strong foundation for his projects? He has to know if the structure is on solid ground. He has to know the laws and regulations related to construction. His contract requires a time for completion and all issues concerning safety. Then I thought of the Creation as worded in the Book of Genesis of the Bible and how the Master Contractor created the universe.

The Master Contractor knew all the laws of construction because he created the laws. He had a plan for how his creation would appear in his eyes. Light and darkness, creatures that crawled, walked and flew, land of various types, and various plants for beauty and food. The Master Contractor designed a universe of strength and growth. He even allowed for team collaboration with the creation of Adam and Eve. With a plan for completion of his project, he gave everything to us free of charge. Wow, what a contractor!.

Because of his massive construction he asked only three things of us: love him, obey him, and love our neighbors. Someone this powerful asked so little of us. He said he would be with us forever and fulfill our every need. He made many promises to us, yet we made no promises to him. He gave us free will, but our misuse of it has consequences. He is the father of all fathers who picks us up when we fall. He made 7,487 promises to us according to the Bible. We can hardly make one promise to him.

Over and over again we show signs of not loving him. Not obeying his rules as a tenant on this earth and we treat our neighbors with disrespect. The 7,487 promises he has given to mankind represent how many times we should forgive others and he is still forgiving us for our everyday sins. He continues to build a foundation that supports us during the worst of times. He continues to build a house in his heavenly world. Will we have paid the mortgage for our heavenly house in order to occupy it?

The Three Hinges

Some may think I'm a little touched in the head, but I have thoughts I want to share with others and I believe these thoughts come from God. This thought came to me when looking at the hinges of my bedroom door. It came to me that we have doors in our homes that have three hinges for a purpose. To me, they represent the Trinity. How am I relating this to the Trinity? Well, I thought the three hinges represented the Father, the Son, and the Holy Spirit and the hinges give spiritual support and an opening that allows us to pass through. As we pass through the doors it represents our journey through life. The journey may be smooth or bumpy.

How many doors do you have in your home with three hinges? If we think about how many doors there are in our homes, this is how many times we should recognize the power of the Three Persons who are opening doors that allow our hearts' desires to become reality. When the doors close we may need privacy. This is the time to personally recognize the Three Persons are always with us, giving us grace and mercy. These are the Three who close the doors on confusion while removing doubts about our lives. They are the Three who want us to love and depend on them.

When we open or close these doors, the Three are watching us. Once a door is closed we have to remember there may be chapters in our lives we want to forget. We also need to repent for past indiscretions. The closed door reminds us God has forgiven us while an open door is a symbol of new opportunities. This is a chance to make things right. The Three Persons through prayer help carry the crosses of life as they guide us to avoid obstacles. Look at the three hinges on your doors and know that the Father, Son and the Holy Spirit are with you as you travel toward salvation. This is just my mental thought, but it reminds me of who has the power and the spiritual light I can share with others. Can you visualize and share this thought with me?

We Are the Trees

I often look at trees and relate their branches to praying hands. Even the lowest branches find a way to reach toward the light. In every season their branches are ever reaching toward the sky. Their barks and trunks are strong and hard as their roots feed from the earth. When winds blow, they still attempt to reach toward the heavens. They may be bent during a storm, but they still remain upright when the storm passes. If the winds are so strong they cause the trees to fall, roots remain to bring new life.

As Christians we are like the trees, sometimes being bent by the troubles of the world, sometimes being broken by the storms of life, yet our faith keeps us reaching up to our Heavenly Father. In the winter months the leaves disappear to store food while the branches keep reaching up. Birds and insects find a safe haven in the trees. Though some insects damage and kill a tree, it stands firm until it has no life. This is how far faith must go. Believing until our end.

Very seldom will I speak of the evil one because he has no power over us if we know the Father, Son, and the Holy Spirit. We bend and may be broken, but God said that there is life after death to bring us peace and joy. We must keep reaching toward the heavens and acknowledge without shame, we follow the words of the Lord.

Our seasons may change, but our faith is stored within us to change situations and people through help from God, the Deliverer. We are fed and guided by Biblical truth. The Master created us with the strength of trees. We are the bark wrapped strongly in his arms. We are the roots bound to his words for nourishment. We are the boughs that continually reach toward heaven. We are the leaves that are renewed by his grace.

V

LEARNING

The Power of Prayer

A friend told me she had been praying to God to build a fence around her for protection against those who wished her evil. As she continued this daily prayer she still had reservations of God's willingness to protect her. Later one night, she dreamed she saw the most beautiful snake. People in the dream were enticed to touch the snake and they died instantly. The gorgeous colors drew people to the snake causing their demise. The snake kept circling the dreamer with eyes glowing. For some unknown reason the dreamer stood as still as she could and the snake turned to slither away. There was an invisible wall the snake could not penetrate. As the dreamer awoke she knew God was responding to her prayer and she later discovered the situation that was causing her pain had vanished.

God always answers our prayers and responds in **his** time. He answers through a dream, other people, and through a thought implanted in the mind. This action of our Lord verifies he is with us at all times. He knows our needs and still supplies them, but it begins with our faith in him. Reading the Bible is an automatic growth tonic because it contains all the spiritual vitamins and minerals we need to sustain us.

When God sent his son to deliver us from sin this was a new beginning for us. Every word and every action of our Lord was a certified check of redemption. It will be cashed on the day of our separation from the physical to the heavenly life with him.

Though I am not a biblical scholar, I do know the power of prayer and I try not to be selfish about my prayers. As a song says, " I pray for you. You pray for me." and our world becomes a better place to share. Prayer also causes one to act. It gives vitality to the spirit.

Faith and a Mustard Seed

Have you ever wondered what the size of a mustard seed really is? Well, its size is about 1 millimeter which is equal to .0394 inches. When Jesus asks us to have the faith the size of a mustard seed, he is not asking much of us. To illustrate faith, the story I like most from the Bible is when Jesus stilled the storm. You know the story too, but let's review it. The story tells us much about our own fears and tribulations and how much control we think we have over unwanted challenges.

The Sea of Galilee lies 695 feet below sea level resting between hills that cause air to funnel. As the air is funneled, dangerously strong wind gusts suddenly occur causing boats to sink. Four of Jesus' disciples were fishermen (Peter, Andrew, James, and John) and were familiar with these storms, but this storm seemed worse than most. The powerful winds and the towering waves caused water to flood the boat. Jesus had dismissed the crowd of five thousand he had miraculously fed with bread and fish.

He then wanted to join the disciples aboard the boat. He walked on the water of swirling waves without sinking. The disciples thought he was a ghost. Jesus in a loud voice told them who he was. Peter was so bold he asked if he could come to Jesus by walking on the waters, too. As Peter walked he began to doubt the command of Jesus to come to Him. Peter began to sink and cried for Jesus to save him. Did Peter have the faith the size of a mustard seed? The disciples had seen all the miracles of Jesus: curing the sick and the lame, raising the dead, feeding a multitude with three fish and five loaves of bread. The mustard seed lesson sank with Peter's fear.

The reference to the mustard seed is a strong reminder, we control nothing. When trials and tribulations come, we must believe our Master is in charge of all things and all situations. Go pray to ask for strength as we contend with problems. With prayer and total faith, we have a whip in our hands that can beat down any troubles. Together they cause struggles to become inconveniences we can kick to the curb. The size of the mustard seed also tells us total faith is a direct path to heaven. We get from God exactly what we desire from him. Proverbs 29:25 states the fear of man lays a snare, but he who trusts in the Lord is safe. I'd rather be safe than caught in a snare.

Love Your Enemies

Years ago this had been the most difficult article to write. I had been attempting to write this for many weeks and even talking about it was difficult. I had issues with some people who were mean-spirited and they seemed like they would be that way forever. It had been hard for me to pray for them, but since I wrote this article I had done something to correct my negative attitude toward them. These seven people needed my prayers and the power of the Holy Spirit to change them.

Loving your enemies was a mouthful for God to say to his children when they had been hurt through words and deeds. Well, I had to remember that Jesus was hurt the same way by many more than seven. It was funny that the number seven was supposed to be a lucky number? I guess it was lucky because it was my gift of tribulation. If I was to become a better person I needed to ask for guidance to change my attitude toward them. My basic concern was my own pride that created fear in my spirit of having to apologize for the things I had said about them after they made me angry. To me, another word for pride was fear: fear of being embarrassed, fear the apology would not be accepted, fear that the person would tell me a thing or two, and fear that they would not apologize for their actions and words toward me. It was funny how tough I was with false pride. I am being very honest, I was just plain scared. It wasn't pride, it was down right fear.

I wrote to the leader of the pack in a letter telling her I was not her enemy. When I gave her the letter in hand to make sure she received it, I felt free. I also wrote that both of us were made in the image of God and I wanted his image to glow outside of me. She came to me still angry and remained so for months, but I still felt free. I did what God wanted me to do. This was my attempt to love an enemy and be free of anger.

Each of us battles the demons of pride, anger, and fear. The devil loves confusion and we must not let hum cause fear in our lives. God made a covenant with us if we leaned on him. I wake up attempting to be a better person than the day before and I'm still trying. It's a **job!** Let us pray for each other to become better than the day before. Fear prevents this when we want to see ourselves as winners and controllers. "Baby bye." was a slang meaning to go sit yourself down somewhere and regroup. If we are truly Christians then we must regroup. Love your enemies and pray for them. They still have to pay consequences for wrong doing, but not from us. But, can we go through the gates of heaven with false pride, anger and fear?

Resolutions

As each New Year passes, there is sometimes a resolution or pledge you make to yourself. You pledge not to eat pork while a fried pork chop sits on your plate with a hot biscuit and spicy gravy. It smells good and your taste buds begin to sing a familiar song - "Gimme that." You vow to go to the gym at least twice a week to lose weight, but after you come from each session at the gym there is a chocolate covered or glazed doughnut hanging from your mouth then you lick your fingertips. You say to yourself I won't eat one next time. Ha! You drive past your favorite restaurant and someone gave you a gift card for Christmas to this restaurant. You can't resist. You push through the doors and order from the menu rich foods that smell good, look good and will taste good. After the meal the waiter asks if you want dessert, you loosen your clothes around your stomach and say YES! You make more resolutions for the New Year than you make to God, and if you did make a resolution to him how long would you keep the promise?

God kept his promises he has made to us. He never forgets these promises, nor is he distracted from his promises by something that feels good, looks good, smells good, and tastes good. Let's look at a few of promises he made to us:

> 1. Eternal Life. 2. Forgiveness. 3. Gift of the Holy Spirit. 4. Supply Needs. 5. Healing (spiritual and physical). 6. Help overcome Temptation. 7. Protection. 8. Deliverance from Fear.

The first is the gift of eternal life. Who do you know who can give anyone eternal life? Only God has this power and his Son died to ensure the peace of eternal life. Second, he forgives our mistakes made in life. Third, the promise that the Holy Spirit would be within us to guide us toward the Light of the World. Sometimes the Holy Spirit is traveling one way while we want to travel elsewhere. Fourth, he supplies our needs from the simple to the complex. Our supplied needs become our blessings. Fifth, he has the power to heal the spirit, mind, and body and when he calls us to leave this world it is a healing. Sixth, he helps us overcome temptation if we truly want his help. Temptations are around us daily like a bird on our shoulders shouting in our ear "Do It". Seventh, he can deliver us from our enemies and protect us when our enemies are upon us. Eight, he delivers us from fear that weakens our spirit and devours the faith we should have.

We are all sojourners on this road toward eternal life. We don't know where or the time of Judgement. As situations and people try to divert us from him, he stands firm on his promises to us and will judge us fairly. We are all sinners, but the best thing in this life is the Master Planner has a plan for all of us. He knows we are sometimes weak, but our superhero is God, our Father, who comes to our rescue. Let's resolve to make him a promise we can keep. Our minds, spirit, and body will be strengthened as the Holy Spirit guides us home.

My Sheep Know Me

Have you ever noticed how a baby follows the voice of the mother and father? The baby learns the sound of the voices of both parents and sometimes can only be comforted by one or both. When someone wants to hold the baby there are loud cries that cause the holder to return the baby to the parent. The baby will follow the voices of the parents with their eyes, locating the parent by sound and a visual presence. The sheep of a shepherd responds the same as a baby. When a parent holds the baby close there is warmth and a strength that is transferred to the baby as it grows. The nearness of the shepherd assures the sheep of their well-being.

The shepherd during the time of Jesus was the caretaker for the sheep. Without the shepherd the sheep could be easily led and killed by predators. Sometimes the shepherd would sing to the sheep to calm them during oncoming storms and when pacing predators were nearby. The shepherd would also fight off the predators as a lone warrior with his staff. He led the sheep to water and to the luscious grasses for grazing. He had total responsibility for the care of the sheep. Just as a baby recognizes the voice of its parents the same occurs as the sheep recognizes his shepherd. Both look to be fed, protected, and comforted.

"The Lord is my shepherd…" is the beginning prayer of Psalm 23 in our Bible. It describes him as our caretaker. Our shepherd knows us and we should certainly know him. He knew us when we were created, born and grew to make choices that sometimes did not include him. We have been led away from our Shepherd by temptations that become attractive. Even when we left the flock he continued to keep the predators from destroying us. Our Shepherd searches for us to bring us back for his protection. He carried us on his shoulders to remind us how much we are loved. There are many pictures of Jesus carrying a sheep on his shoulders. Jesus wrapped it around His shoulders whispering in the ear of the sheep and probably singing a melody to calm it. They also felt the warmth of his spirit and the strength in his shoulders. Indeed, he is our "refuge and our strength."

Our Shepherd leads us to the still waters as we thirst for his goodness. When we walk toward danger he is the lonesome warrior fighting for our salvation. Such a shepherd, as our Lord, is a reminder he is always with us even when we go astray. He will find us to give us unceasing love. He is the Shepherd who loves providing for our daily needs, forgiving our trespasses when we forgive others and ourselves. We need to follow this Shepherd because he never goes back on his promises. Let him carry you on his shoulders to truly know him. Listen to the voice and follow. He knows you. Why not know him?

Our Anchor

An anchor is a strong device that is released from a vessel to touch the bottom of a body of water. It holds the vessel in place to keep it from drifting due to the winds and currents. The anchor supports the vessel and prevents its passengers from unexpected dangers during a storm. Do we know we are on a vessel called life with an anchor always supporting us? As we travel on this vessel, we were given a strong and powerful anchor.

When storms arrive to cause us to drop to our knees, the Anchor is there to pull us to our feet. When our mind is in turmoil, the Anchor gives us peace. When we feel there is no hope, the Anchor opens doors aboard our vessel no one else can open. When there are financial problems, our Anchor provides our lottery. When we feel cowardly, our Anchor supplies us with courage. Our Anchor is so powerful we need not fear the storms we encounter. Our Anchor is with us through all our tornados, hurricanes, and tsunamis. Our Anchor is a son named Jesus.

Our Anchor is with us just as he was when Peter felt he could walk on water. Then Peter's faith dwindled and he began to sink. He yelled for Jesus to save him. Jesus did just that and reminded Peter he had little faith. A storm occurred while Jesus was asleep on a boat with his apostles. It became so hazardous the apostles awakened Jesus shaking with fear. Their Anchor stood and calmed the storm. These two examples of Jesus saving his apostles proves he is always with us no matter how bumpy the ride. Our faith must be as strong as his love for us. He is truly our ANCHOR as we travel our ship of life.

The Old and The New

God gave us the Ten Commandments to remind us of the various temptations that prevent us from obeying and loving him. These commandments were given to Moses as part of the Old Testament. But there is another set of rules we often forget. Do you remember! These are the ten laws we seldom lean on for strength and forgiveness. These laws were spoken by Jesus on Mount Sinai. The Ten Commandments and the Beatitudes are considered the Old and the New Laws of faith. Through the Beatitudes, Jesus encourages us how to live to fulfill the Ten Commandments. The Beatitudes tell us the importance of character:

1. If we are **poor in spirit** we shall be comforted. Jesus speaks of spiritual poverty. When we accept God in our lives we are assured of eternal life.
2. When we **mourn** it is not a childish self-pity. It is a deep sorrow for our sins and repentance for them. Sin hurts others, as well as,ourselves. God knows our pain and will turn it into joy.
3. We will inherit the earth when we are **meek**. Meekness is yielding to God and making him your Lord and Master.
4. When we **hunger and thirst** for righteousness there is an awesome need to know God. Being a community of Christians means we are searching for truth and the truth is God.
5. When we **show mercy** we will receive the grace and mercy from God. We must show forgiveness, kindness, and compassion to others.
6. If we have **a pure heart**, God guarantees we will be with him in heaven. He can see we are cleansing ourselves from within through daily prayer.

7. We can become **peacemakers** who live in peace and help preserve peace. This brings together the fellowship of man.
8. When **persecuted** because we seek our Father of righteousness, we can exhibit our faith rather than hide it.
9. If we are **insulted, persecuted, and evil words are spoken against us**, we need not be afraid because God will fight our battles.
10. If we **rejoice** when we follow the laws of Jesus we will have exemplified the prophets who were persecuted because they preached the New Law. /they joyfully died for Christ.

As a former educator I know the importance of having rules in schools. Rules help to build character and learn the importance of responsibilities. This is the same for the Ten Commandments and the Beatitudes. Each balances off the other. The Ten Commandment are the rules of life and the Beatitudes build character.

"Thy Will Be Done"

After being discharged from the hospital on September 16, 2022, I came home feeling sorry for myself. I was asking myself "Why me?" and a voice answered "Why not you?" God didn't make me sick. I brought some of my illnesses upon myself. When I was young I didn't think about the future and how actions have repercussions. Then while sitting on the side of my bed, I remembered a gospel song: **Take Me to the King by Tamala Mann** that struck my mind. The words of the refrain are "Take me to the King. I don't have much to bring. My heart is torn to pieces. It's my offering." Is this the offering I have given to God? He has given me so much and I have given him so little in comparison. When a challenge comes to hit me on the head with a hammer, I want to be taken to the King. Then I also remembered Abraham, when he was told to sacrifice his son. Abraham did exactly what God told him to do and because of his obedience God abandoned his original demand. Abraham's faith was tested. Abraham did the will of God.

When we say the **Our Father,** do the words have true meaning to us? Are we really focused on the significance of the words? Do we realize that the first words of this prayer are to a power greater than our own? Do we know we are promising that his will should be done as long as we have life? Do we know how often he forgives us our sins? He gives us everything he knows we need. How grateful we should be. Again, he has given us so much and we have given him so little. Have we really thought about the abundance given us in our daily lives? The final question on the day of judgment will probably be if we did the will of God, or were we haphazard about doing his will?

God gave us the Ten Commandments to live by. The first three tell us about our duties to him. The other seven concern our compassion and respect to our neighbors. He has given us a pathway to his kingdom, yet, we cannot even remember the Ten Commandments. We are his creations who sometimes forget who gave us life. Let's not forget to constantly do his will knowing his will has power and consequences while our will is as frail as a feather.

Good Friday Reflection

At noon on Good Friday I began saying my prayers to commemorate the Crucifixion of Jesus Christ. In my mind I saw those standing in pain at the bottom of the Cross. The apostle John, Mary the mother of Jesus, Mary Magdalene and Mary Cleofas stood with hearts broken. They were in dismay at the cruel death of Jesus who had not committed any crimes. I wondered if I would have been a follower of Christ standing at the bottom of the Cross or would I have been an accuser who shouted to crucify him. His death brought to mind also how much good he had done for the people of his time. Why kill a man who displayed only kindness to others? He cured the blind, the lame walked, healed the sick, changed water into wine and many other miracles as recorded in the books of Matthew, Luke, Mark, and John.

The apostles didn't seem to remember his teachings to them. Not one of them was standing at the bottom of the Cross. He reminded them he would not be with them forever, but they would be protected, yet, only one of them was at the foot of the Cross. They were hiding like cowards. They were afraid that what happened to Jesus would happen to them. **Oh, men of little faith.** Would I have been hiding with them? They abandoned him and did not truly believe until they saw him after his Resurrection. Until Jesus stood before them did they believe this was the Son of God. He really made chumps of them all.

This was a brutal way to die. Hanging on a cross with the sensitive parts of the body pierced with nails. Would I have been able to hang like this for three hours or more until I died? Did Jesus also wonder where the apostles were or did he already know what they would do? The question today is what would I have done and what would you have done? We gained the greatest gift. Salvation for us was gained by a bloody sacrifice. Would we die for a member of our family or for a friend? Jesus is part of our family and a friend. May we have the strength to openly and faithfully stand as a follower of Christ without hesitation? Think about it. **Are we chumps?**

VI

MY WORLD

He Made Me Black

God made me black. For what reasons I don't know, but he had a reason. All I know is how my ancestors survived a life of enslavement for 400 years in America. In 1447 a Portuguese ship approached the shores of Africa and kidnapped twelve men taking them from Africa to Portugal. The slave trade began. From the 1490's to 1685 the countries involved in the slave trade were Portugal, Spain, England, France, Holland, Sweden, Denmark and Germany. The people of these countries believed in the inferiority of black Africans.Why did God allow this to happen to a population of man's first civilization, I don't know. But God has allowed me to take pride in my history of challenges.

The challenges they faced were challenges they wanted their children to avoid. New challenges have arisen since laws were enacted to eradicate slavery, but still racism continues. It is still a major concern of black and brown people, yet people of color still struggle to show their worth. The one thing I know is we must keep God in our lives. As an individual, I know God loves me by the obstacles he removes from my life's journey, and the joys he brings to me. Why God made me black I do not care because he is in my life.

In 1956 a professor at Stanford University, William Shockley, the 1956 Nobel Prize winner for Physics, theorized that black people were inherently less intelligent than whites. This caused an uproar among black people and especially black students. He added that welfare was a waste of time for blacks since their IQ's were less than 100, therefore, they should be sterilized. Can you see how God worked against Shockley's theories? Look at the number of black doctors, in various fields of medicine, inventors, astronauts, educators, athletes, architects, pilots, students attending college, a President of the United States, and so many other areas. Black women are currently the most educated population in the United States. God made me black to ensure I never doubted my abilities and his love. Everything a racist says about blacks can be disproved.

Why God made me black I will never know. One true fact is the earth population of black and brown people is three fourths of the world's population. Why God made me black is a question that will never be answered in this life. I just try to live a life God would say, " Good job, Old Girl! I saw your growth over the years that led you to my house. You have loved me, as I have loved you".

Here I Come World

Here I am, World!

whether you want me or not.

I come with a vitality to conquer the impossible.

I come with an assurance that things can change for the best.

Here I come, World,

as significant as the aesthetic beauty surrounding me.

I come with compassion for my fellow man needing
understanding where it is lacking.

I come with love that is patient, non-argumentative and unending.

Here I come, World, ready or not!

I Came

I came into this world screaming and crying.

I came into a world of blue skies, green grass, and air so sweet

I came into a world where I was loved by a family, strong and proud.

I came into a world troubled by World War II.

I came into a world where in elementary school we searched for Korea on our classroom map because there was another war.

I came into the world when my loving husband was drafted to fight in the jungles of VietNam.

I came into the world to populate it with a child I bore and who is a Krystal Joy.

I came into this world to lift spirits through teaching children who looked like me to let them know they could reach for the stars.

I came into this world with a purpose only God knew at the time, but my purpose he planned has always been to fight for freedom of mind and body.

I came into a world still sometimes screaming and crying, but that was to make a better way for the next generation.

I came into the world to leave a memory of what good I tried to do, hoping I did my best for those I touched.

I will probably leave a world in need of clean water and air, land, and the hearts of people who call earth their home.

My last good-bye will only be the word PEACE.

Just Me

Whom do I want to be, while the years require me to participate in a world which doubts me?

Who can I be as I look into my ancestral heritage as a means to maintain most of my culture?

Who can I be as I fantasize my social, political, and economic future?

Am I all that strange to look at?

Am I all that different that no one sees me?

Am I *all that misunderstood that I cannot dream without doubting my own abilities?*

Look at me! Take a good look.

Skin the color of the enriched earth, eyes the color of profundity, a body straight and strong, a mind cognizant of ethics and justice.

Look at me! I have dreams worth fighting for and dreams which will become reality.

Look at me! I'm me.

My Heritage

My African heritage is something I respect and love. The greatest reason for my respect and love is because God made me the way he wanted me to be. God made my people beautiful to complement their lush environment. My African heritage comes from a continent full of rich natural resources and topographical beauty. The people are a celebration of God's magnificent diversity of black and brown colors. But my heritage has also been a history of disrespect by others who enslaved them, divided original tribal lands, and colonized their territories.

My heritage led my ancestors to an unfamiliar land where they were stripped of their language, culture, religion, and self-respect. For four-hundred years my ancestors were slaves to people who used the Bible as an excuse for keeping their minds and bodies in bondage. The true history of my heritage are the centuries before Jesus Christ lived. This information is not the applauded accolades my heritage deserves. My enemies would rather make me think I had no authentic history. Yet, my heritage is the presence of my people who had kings and queens and supremacy over sovereign kingdoms. My history is a trilogy of enslavement, racism, and battles for equality overcome because of my Creator.

I write this article because God and my ancestors have given me a toughness to survive. This constantly reminds me my creation is in the image of God. My Creator is the master sculptor who forms each one of us as distinct individuals. My mom told me of the garden of God that was a collection of the most beautiful flowers with different scents and different colors. Some grow very tall while others grow close to the ground, but each had a purpose. She told me I was one of the flowers and my sister Tish was another type of flower. As we grew, we would find our purpose in the garden. My mom was perceptive and wise. She was God's partner who bolstered my faith with her words.

Black History is not just for February, but an all year-long study and appreciation of my sculptors. My God and my ancestors molded a person who would sometimes fall, but always rise to see the world as it is. With this vision, my God taught me to see worldly possibilities and strive to change things needing change and to love those created in his image just as I am. If I have been created by God, I have a purpose to fulfill in life. I'm not perfect, but he continues to remold me as I am sometimes damaged on my journey. If my mind is muddled, he restores orderly thoughts. When I'm ill he breathes new breath into me. My body may have scars, but they are just a reminder I'm healed.

So, when we look at each other, remember we have a common ancestry and a heritage that extends centuries. When we look at each other we are the flowers in God's garden. When we look at each other, our Creator is a father with many children of different colors. When we look at each other let us see God.